TRAINING YOUR PUPPY

JACK DIAMOND

© T.F.H. Publications, Inc.

Distributed in the UNITED STATES to the Pet Trade by T.F.H. Publications, Inc., 1 TFH Plaza, Neptune City, NJ 07753; on the Internet at www.tfh.com; in CANADA by Rolf C. Hagen Inc., 3225 Sartelon St., Montreal, Quebec H4R 1E8; Pet Trade by H & L Pet Supplies Inc., 27 Kingston Crescent, Kitchener, Ontario N2B 2T6; in ENGLAND by T.F.H. Publications, PO Box 74, Havant PO9 5TT; in AUSTRALIA AND THE SOUTH PACIFIC by T.F.H. (Australia), Pty. Ltd., Box 149, Brookvale 2100 N.S.W., Australia; in NEW ZEALAND by Brooklands Aquarium Ltd., 5 McGiven Drive, New Plymouth, RD1 New Zealand; in SOUTH AFRICA by Rolf C. Hagen S.A. (PTY.) LTD., P.O. Box 201199, Durban North 4016, South Africa; in JAPAN by T.F.H. Publications. Published by T.F.H. Publications, Inc.
MANUFACTURED IN THE
UNITED STATES OF AMERICA
BY T.F.H. PUBLICATIONS, INC.

These American Eskimo puppies are ready and willing to learn anything you have to teach them.

CONTENTS

PHOTO CREDITS:
ISABELLE FRANCAIS, ROBERT PEARCY AND VINCE SERBIN

Most puppies, like this Boxer, are astute and able pupils.

INTRODUCTION

Dogs hold a place in human history equaled by no other animal. They have worked with humans as the centuries have come and gone. However, because of our tremendous familiarity with dogs, many owners assume they know how to train them without understanding the way they think and learn. Alas, the folly of such an assumption is clear from the growing numbers of animals abandoned by irresponsible owners each year.

There are then those owners who recognize the tremendous pleasure that can be derived from a highly trained canine. They invest a great deal of their time into studying training techniques so their dogs will fulfill single or multi-purpose roles—shepherding, hunting, advanced obedience tests, rescue work, and the like.

Most owners are everyday people who are true dog lovers and want a pet to share their lives with. They are responsible and want a pet that will be "man's best friend." Unfortunately, they accept a relationship that, in many areas, falls well short of what it could be if they would take the time to properly train their canine companion. It is for these owners that this book was written.

Training a puppy does not take a very long time—perhaps a few months. In that time, the cute little bundle of fun and mischief you first took home will develop into a wonderful pet that will be your pride and joy. Without proper training, your relationship with your dog will be unfulfilling for both of you, as well as, at times, upsetting, embarrassing, and downright frustrating! Just a few problems commonly seen in dogs can be corrected quickly and kindly in the first few training sessions. You will be surprised to find that a

Dogs have held a place in human history for centuries. Because of this, many owners assume they know how to train them.

formerly unruly family member will suddenly become a model citizen.

Training should begin in the first few weeks of your puppy's residency at his new home. So now the question becomes—where to begin? What your puppy grows up to be as an adult is a direct reflection of the time and attention you afforded him during his developmental days.

Training should begin in the first few weeks of your puppies residency at your home.

Proper training techniques will help your pup to live a full life.

In the following chapters you will learn to appreciate your dog for who he is and how he thinks. Once you better understand these aspects, you will find training your puppy is simple as long as you are consistent and use your new found knowledge wisely. Within days of beginning training you will see progress; within weeks your puppy will be delighting you with what he has learned; within months you will have accomplished what many fail to do; and for the rest of your dog's life you will enjoy a bond of mutual affection and trust. All this from the few weeks of basic training you invested—a very small investment for the problems it avoids.

The following chapters provide information you will need to apply once training is underway. This book will teach you how to communicate with your puppy, and understand how he learns, avoiding problems, and helping to make training an enjoyable experience for you both.

How Your Puppy's Mind Works

When you invite a puppy into your home he becomes a member of the family.

In many soceieties today pets are held in high esteem—considered members of the family. From an early age we are, through fables, stories, movies and books, encouraged to believe the characters in them can talk and think as we do. The proof of this can be heard in things many dog owners say. Examples include: "He didn't mean to do that," "He knows he shouldn't do that," "He understands everything I say." Somewhere along the line we forget that our dog is not human, and therefore doesn't think like one.

In order to succesfully understand your pet, you must clear your mind of the tendency to apply human thinking to your puppy. Instead, accept him for what he actually is—a once wild animal. A succesful trainer will merely modify, or channel, your puppy's natural inclinations and behavior patterns into those acceptable in a human society. Luckily, dogs fit in very well with human families because they mirror, in many ways, the lifestyle of the wild dog's social structure—he will merely begin to see the family as his pack.

To successfully understand your pet, accept him for what he is.

Remember, when you take a puppy into your home you are expecting him to live by your rules, not those he would live by in the wild. Suprisingly, even today, dogs still rely on instinct more than we would expect. Making your puppy a good family member may take some time, but with patient training and plenty of tender loving care, your puppy will strive to please you.

THE DOG PACK

The wild dog pack displays a social organization that compares most closely with a hierarchal system. In order to truly understand your puppy, it is helpful to understand and respect the system. Dog packs have a single leader. He or she have their "close friends," who have their friends, and on and on, until

Dogs fit in very well with families. She will begin to view the family as her pack.

Even though dogs have been domesticated for centuries, they still rely a great deal on instinct. Pack mentality plays a role in your dog's relationships to other animals as well as to humans.

order that works towards survival, and the growth of the pack.

The key aspects of pack life are: it is based on an order of dominance; members will always be trying to improve their status; a pup is taught by all members of the pack, instilling respect; pups are not taught by reason, but by consistent discipline, and success in their pack role.

The mind of a dog is geared toward life as part of a social organization in which he respects the power of those capable of exerting authority. This authority is essential to the survival of the pack. From it, comes the organization needed to tackle prey larger than the dog himself. If an individual senses that a higher ranked member is incapable of exerting

we reach the lower ranks, comprising of the weakest individuals. Pups are born into a given status, depending on their parents. But there is always a competitive situation in which the lowly seek to move upwards, either by befriending higher status members, or by proving they are tougher than such members. The structure of the pack is thus one that favors those in power, yet enables an especially tough or clever youngster to improve his place in the hierarchy.

The pack is never a totally static unit. Youngsters grow older and challenge the strongest, or those in the highest positions. The young puppy is taught by all pack members what is, and what is not, acceptable. By the time a pup is old enough to hunt, he has been fully educated in the social rules of the pack. There are no exceptions to this, offenders are always disciplined in one form or another. When the youngster is taken on hunts he will

learn by observation where he should be in relation to other pack members. He will learn which animals are prey, which are not, and how they should be tracked and attacked. The result is an

At one time all your puppy's needs would have been met by members of his pack. Now you will have to see to them, including his grooming. Your puppy will need a special brush depending on his coat length or skin condition. There are slicker brushes, pin brushes, curry brushes— something to suit the needs of any dog. Photo courtesy of Four Paws.

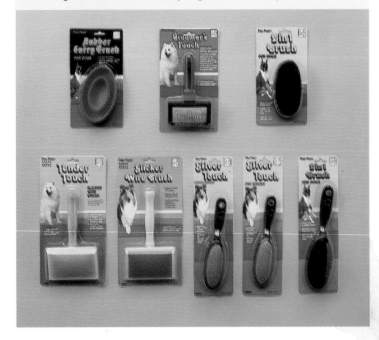

As a young member of a pack a puppy will be taught by all members what is and is not acceptable behavior. In order for this young Newfoundland to feel safe and secure in your home you must establish yourself as pack leader.

In order to grow up and fit in with a family it is essential that any puppy be given a sound education and be treated in a consistent manner.

authority he will challenge that member until he usurps his position.

To the wild dog every day is a battle in which he must play his part in ensuring the success of the hunt if he wishes to eat, reproduce, and thus survive. The wild pack is under constant despotic rule. On the contrary, once a puppy matures and understands the rules, his life can be as pleasant as possible. His leader does not display an inconsistent attitude, nor do other pack members. There are always squabbles within the pack that constantly work to maintain the status quo of rank.

Obviously, life for a puppy in a human pack is quite different than that of his wild relatives. To be able to grow up and fit in with a human family, it is absolutely essential that he be given a sound education, be treated in a consistent manner, and is aware of his position in the pack. Basic training and behavior modification, as discussed in the following chapters of this book, will help in getting your puppy familiar with family life. Remember, dogs have been domesticated for thousands of years, it is not as if you are bringing a wolf into your home. However, puppies are mischievious, active, energetic creatures that need your attention and direction.

Puppies, like these St. Bernards are mischievous, active, energetic creatures that need your attention and direction.

THE LEARNING PROCESS

Your puppy learns by a combination of the following: observation, hearing, reactions to stimuli, and memory recall, as well as instinct. Instinct is something every animal is born with—a subconscious involuntary ability to react in a given way without having to apply any conscious thought to the matter. It is a safety valve, a means that helps all animals to survive when they have no previous experiences to draw from. Instinct can be overridden by memory because it gives the animal alternative choices based on the consequences of past actions. In the absence of experiences, an animal will always react in an instinctive manner.

COMMON MISTAKES IN BEGINNING TRAINING

Before training your puppy, understand that your weaknesses can effect a pup as he matures into a dog. The most common error is to assume the puppy fully understands what you say. He is able to associate certain word sounds to required actions. The tone of the voice, and facial expressions, are also important in helping the puppy to understand the requirement of the word, and its context.

For these reasons, words used in training should be short, never sentences. Hand signals must always be quite clear and distinct from any other signal that might convey a totally different

Before beginning training, remember that your behavior as "pack leader" greatly affects your puppy. Impatience and inconsistency will hinder your efforts.

requirement. Another concern is inconsistency. If a given behavior pattern is or is not acceptable there must be no variation in your reaction to it. You cannot allow your puppy to sleep on a chair one day, but not on the next. You must never call your puppy to you and then apply discipline, having given praise on other occasions.

Also, remember you can not discipline a dog in the present for something done in the past, and expect he will understand why he is being disciplined. He will associate the discipline with the most recent thing he did—usually coming to you. These common mistakes are the recipe for a confused dog. Unfortunately, many owners seem unable to understand these realities, and unwittingly make training more difficult.

Training your puppy will be much easier once you fully understand how your puppy learns.

LEARNING BY STIMULI

All life forms react to stimuli—which is any thing, or action, that elicits a response—in one of three predictable ways. Reaction is either positive, neutral (passive), or negative. In some situations there is no neutral situation. For example, when walking your dog and you tell him to stop, he either stops or keeps going, there is no potential for a neutral reaction. If the dog stops, your reaction will be either positive (praise), or neutral (you do nothing). If he does not stop, your reaction will be negative (you physically bring the dog to a halt). These reactions to stimuli are a vital part of the learning process. Continuing with the example, logic tells you that your dog would rather come to a halt and gain praise than continue walking and elicit your displeasure.

If your dog keeps walking in this situation it may be

Your puppy learns by a combination of observation, hearing, reacting, memory and instinct.

because he has not grasped the notion that when you stop he is expected to stop(in which case you have failed to communicate the needed response to a given stimuli), or because he is ignoring your stopping action because something ahead is more appealing than the discomfort he associates with your displeasure. However, if you praise the dog one time for

When training never react differently to the same situation. Your reaction to a puppy's behavior must always be consistent.

stopping, then discipline him the next time, you should not be surprised if the dog becomes totally confused. You must never react in two opposing ways to the same situation. Your reaction to an action of the puppy must always be positive (or neutral) or negative, never both. If this happens, you deny the puppy the opportunity to learn which action is expected of him. You become a poor teacher, and will end up with a poor pupil. There are no untrainable dogs, just lots of owners unable to train them.

Your puppy will remember the consequences of his actions. When situations arise, your puppy will scan his memory for the proper way to react.

MEMORY

Every time your puppy is confronted with a situation the consequences of his actions are stored in his memory. The next time a similar situation arises the puppy will subconsciously scan his memory for how he should react. Taking a simple example, if you call the puppy to you and give him lots of fuss for coming, that is what he associates with the action of coming. The next time you call, he will come bounding to you with tail wagging and head held high because he associates this action with praise.

Consider now the common reaction seen in many dogs when their owner calls them. It approaches cautiously, sometimes with tail wagging, but low. In sad cases he approaches his owner in a very submissive manner, half crawling, sometimes even urinating. This instantly tells

Puppies are playful and inquisitive creatures. They want to learn what you have to teach them. A well socialized puppy will welcome training sessions.

any observer what's been happening. On some occasions the dog has received fuss when going to his master. On other occasions he has been disciplined for something he did in the past. But the dog does not know this, so he records in his memory that at one time he was punished for going to his master.

We now have two opposing consequences for the same action. Ultimately, the dog does not know what to expect if he obeys the come command. He wants to please his master, so moves towards him or her—but memory recall tells him the consequence of doing so may be unpleasant, so he takes up a submissive posture to display his subordination. He may also react by running away, which usually elicits even more punishment when caught, thus reinforcing the notion that going to his master, or being caught, will result in discipline!

From this simple scenario you should glean two golden rules when training your puppy. The first, if you call the puppy to you, and even if he has wreaked havoc while you were out, he must receive only fuss for coming to you. He lives only for the moment—what he did in the past is now forgotten. Your present command is for him to come to you. If he responds to your wishes, he has done what you want. He must be rewarded, never punished. Secondly, if your puppy does something wrong it is essential that he's disciplined at the moment of the misdemeanor. You must learn that your puppy will not understand you are disciplining him for an act done in the past. You must always think in terms relative to the present moment. It is what happens in the present that will be stored in the puppy's memory and recalled when needed for decision making the next time a situation arises.

If your puppy has done something wrong it is essential that he is corrected at the moment the misdemeanor occurs.

PRAISE & DISCIPLINE

Your puppy learns appropriate behavior through successes that should be rewarded with praise and inappropriate behavior through correction. The severity of discipline applied to a puppy should be minimal—only what is required to suppress an unwanted behavior. Anything more is excessive and unnecessary. The level of discipline can always be increased, but once excessive discipline has been used, negative side effects will occur. Remember, training should be a bonding experience for you and your dog.

From the outset, you must be clear about what behaviors you consider acceptable. Failure to do this can result in confusion and problems as the puppy matures. For example, many owners encourage a puppy to engage in a tug-of-war game with a slipper—after all, you are only playing. However, what you are doing is encouraging the puppy to hold on to things and try to win the tug-of-war game. Will you be so happy to engage in this when the pup has a vice-like grip on your best shoes, or clothing? If you do not want your puppy to sleep on chairs or your bed, don't allow him to do so while he's a puppy. If you do not want him to jump up on people when he is an adult, don't encourage him to do so.

This does not mean your puppy shouldn't be allowed to do "puppy things," but

Be sure to praise your puppy when he behaves in the bath. A wide range of shampoos exist to meet any dog's needs, from flea and tick to specially medicated to whitening and brightening and more. All shampoos are pH balanced for a gentle yet effective cleaning. Photo courtesy of Four Paws.

exercise care in what you actually encourage him to do. Encouragement is a form of praise. It conveys to the puppy that it is acceptable to do this or that. Let him have his own toys— items such as a ball, or Nylabone®, things he will not confuse with items you do not want him to grow up regarding as toys. Play appropriate games, but try not to participate in games in which he is encouraged to bite on your clothes, body, or anything else.

If you don't want your puppy to sleep on the furniture be sure to give him his own comfortable bed or place to go to when he wants privacy. Respect his privacy and teach your children to do likewise. If you do not want him eating a bone on your living room carpet don't let him start doing so. Take him to the kitchen every time he appears in the living room

Your puppy learns appropriate behavior through successes that should be rewarded with praise.

with a bone; and then praise him when he settles down to eat it in the kitchen.

CONSISTENCY IS EVERYTHING

Once you have determined the house rules for your puppy you must apply them consistently all of the time. If you allow even the smallest infraction to continue, unwanted behavior will surely increase. You will never be able to shape the mind of your puppy more easily than while he's a baby. It is always much easier to prevent a problem than finding a cure.

Teach your children to treat your puppy with care and respect. Never allow them to mishandle him, causing undue harm.

Do not allow affection for your puppy to override your common sense or his educational needs. At all times, you must take on the role of parent.

Although it may be difficult because you love your puppy so much, you must take action when necessary. Do not allow affection, or sentimentality, to override

Today's training methods, used consistently with patience will produce a happy and well adjusted canine companion.

Once you have determined rules for your puppy you must apply them all of the time. The easiest time to shape your pet's mind is when he is a puppy.

your common sense, or his educational needs. You must, at all times, take on the role of parent. As soon as you realize an unwanted behavior is developing, act on it. The puppy must do what he's told, it is your responsibility to be sure these things are conveyed to him in a kind and consistent manner.

THE POWER OF YOUR VOICE

"Spare the rod and spoil the dog" and "You sometimes have to be cruel to be kind"—two phrases that hold no place in the training of a puppy—let no one convince you otherwise.

Present knowledge of canine psychology finds that the harsh disciplinary methods of dog training applied in the past are being relegated to history, and with good cause. Today's alternatives are no less effective, and carry far less risk of negative side effects if used consistently, regularly, and with patience.

The most potent training tool you can implement is the power of your voice. Whatever the size or breed of your puppy, it will, as a pup, be small in relation to you. This fact alone places you in a very authoritative position. The

mere tone of your voice will oftentimes be adequate to discipline a puppy. During actual training sessions, restraint, corrections, and your voice, will be your prime training tools.

Your voice, in praise and admonishment, will vary in tone and volume. These subtle changes will achieve more for you than all the training aids put together. It is the most ongoing form of communication you can develop with you dog. Use it wisely and it will enable you to achieve great things with your newly acquired canine family member.

The most powerful training tool you have at your disposal is your voice. The mere tone of your voice will be adequate enough to discipline a puppy.

BONDING WITH YOUR PUPPY

The degree of affection existing between any animal and his owner is a result of their time spent together. The greater the amount of time spent, the stronger their bond will be. Training is often a bonding experience for dogs and their owners. In fact, your success will depend on how strong the bond you have established is. During the bonding period you will be gently establishing your authority as the pack leader and parent, as well as establishing what is and is not acceptable.

TALK AND TOUCH

While you should use a minimum amount of words for specific training commands, the reverse is true when bonding. The more you talk, the more the puppy will gain an understanding of the tone of your voice as a communicative indicator of your mood. Stroking and touching the puppy is also an essential part of the bonding process.

When talking, do so in a soft voice, the puppy will find your voice soothing. As you talk, stroke each part of his body, in particular, stroke the ears, tail, feet and underbelly. Chest scratching is always enjoyable, as is rubbing the area just anterior of the tail. Gently lift the lips and touch the teeth—not an inspection, just a quick look. This is all

part of the subtle process that builds confidence in you. By observing the pup's reaction to being touched in various places you will learn if he has any negatively sensitive areas. Most dogs have at least one area that they do not like to be touched. You must consistently focus attention on this area, your puppy needs to trust you in all things.

HANDLING YOUR PUPPY

The way you handle and play with your puppy is crucial to his trust in you. If

The degree of affection existing between any animal and his owner is a result of the time they spend together. The greater the amount of quality time spent, the stronger the bond.

you do not treat your puppy gently he will recall his contact with you as unpleasant. Never pull on a puppy's ears, legs, or tail. Never pull on the loose skin around his neck, or lift the puppy up by this. When lifting the pup, always place your hand under his chest and bring the pup up to your chest. This way, he will never feel discomfort or insecurity. Do not let children lift the puppy by his front legs so his body is dangling. Always supervise any situation in which your puppy will be held. If you need to restrain your puppy while he's on the ground place one hand in front of his chest, the other over his shoulders—an effective way to stop him without his feeling threatened.

The way you handle and play with your puppy is essential to his trust in you. If you do not treat your puppy gently he will recall his contact with you as unpleasant. Always *handle with care.*

PLAYTIME

All puppies love to play and should be encouraged to do so. Kneel down or lay on the carpet so the pup can clamber over you, roll over, and snuggle up to you—all are important to bonding. Allow your puppy to play how he wants within reason, but do not encourage behavior that has already been deemed unacceptable. Play should not consist of shredding paper, or rummaging in the trash bin. If these things occur, simply lift your puppy up and say "No" in a gentle but firm voice as you move him away. This is gentle discipline involving no punishment. The word no is being used and conveys your displeasure. When playing, try to avoid overexciting your— puppy this may lead to instinctual play habits such as nipping. Instantly, and softly, say "No," remove your hand and bring the game to an end for a few moments. Always provide a puppy with things he is allowed to chew on, like a Nylabone® so he has things to bite on during his teething period.

Try to remember your puppy is still a baby, rough play should have its limits. Do not play roughly with the puppy to the point of frightening him. Do not hide and suddenly jump out at

All puppies love to play and should be encouraged to do so. Playing with your puppy is an important time of bonding and closeness.

your puppy in order to startle him. Innocuous as this may seem, it serves no useful purpose other than to make your puppy more cautious.

BEGINNING EDUCATION

If your puppy is old enough to have been weaned and separated from his mother and siblings, he's old enough to begin his education. This does not mean formal lessons. Rather, you will be training by restraint, and by encouraging appropriate behavior. The word "No" will be well used, but should never take on a harsh tone at this stage. The fact the puppy may not appear to react to the word does not mean it isn't registering in his mind in relation to unwanted actions.

If you see the puppy doing something naughty, never rush at him. This will frighten him into running away from you, the last thing you want. Instead, walk calmly to the puppy, say "No," then lift him up, at which point he will probably want to wash your face, which is fine.

A puppy is never too young to begin his education. This does not necessarily mean formal training. At this point, you will simply be encouraging appropriate behavior.

There are several other behaviors that are important not to encourage. First, if you do not want your puppy to sleep or play on your furniture do not let him play on your lap while you are seated. Kneel on the floor. Secondly, no dog should get into the habit of jumping up.

Do not ever encourage the development of a puppy's bad habits. Once he is a grown dog begging for food at the dinner table will not seem quite so amusing.

Do not ever encourage this behavior. When the puppy attempts to jump at you, step backwards so the attempt fails every time. Finally, do not feed your puppy tidbits from the dinner table, while you are having dinner. This can develop into a bad habit which, in its extreme form, results in stealing from the table. To avoid those doleful eyes and wagging tail, place the puppy in another room while you eat. The temptation for both of you is then removed.

THE FIRST FEW NIGHTS

Unless your puppy is already familiar with sleeping on his own he will miss his mother and siblings and

Your puppy's first few days away from his mother and siblings will be frightening. As long as your puppy is kept warm and well fed, be confident that he will adjust shortly and become familiar with his surroundings.

whimper or howl when left alone. If you do not want sleeping on your bed to become a habit, do not allow your puppy to do so now. Instead, provide a dog bed with warm blankets near your bed, a wind up ticking clock may be helpful if placed near the bed. It simulates the heart beat of his former bed mates and will soothe him. If the puppy whimpers resist the temptation to go to him. As long as the pup is warm and well fed you can be confident that the problem will cease within a day or two as the puppy becomes familiar with his room and surroundings.

COLLAR AND LEAD FAMILIARITY

During the time bonding is taking place, it is a good idea to familiarize the puppy with his collar, choke chain, and lead. No attempts should be made to train, simply to accustom your puppy to the feel of these, and of the restraint a lead creates. Place the collar on the puppy before playing—he will soon forgets he's wearing it. After a short while remove the collar. Repeat this process over a few days and the collar will become a neutral object. Never leave a choke chain on a puppy unless you are present. Once the pup ignores the collar you can attach the lead and walk around the room, letting the puppy go where he wants. Do this when he is quiet and when there no distractions. After this has happened a few times you can encourage the pup to go where you want by calling him to you while applying the gentlest of tugs on the lead.

Never drag the puppy, always coax him. By this gentle process the puppy will learn in a matter of days to walk with you without bucking and pulling. This will be especially beneficial once you commence housebreaking, as well as during training exercises.

As you can see from the examples discussed so far, training can be introduced very gradually as the puppy bonds with the family. There is no pain, or even discomfort, yet the puppy is already being taught to associate simple words with action, as well as learning appropriate behavior through encouragement and restraint.

Training can be a wonderful way to bond with your puppy.

Your first step towards training your puppy should be familiarizing him with his collar and lead; do not attempt to begin training activities.

Training can be introduced as a puppy bonds with his family. There is no stress involved, yet the puppy is already being taught by encouragement and restraint.

YOUR PUPPY'S TEMPERAMENT

A puppy reared in a loving environment with his mother and siblings already has been given a good start in life. This will ensure your puppy's easy adjustment to his new family.

attention to your puppy's personality and behaviors will help you decide on proper training methods.

A PUPPY'S BEGINNINGS

The needs of one puppy may be vastly different to those of another. Every puppy is an individual. In some cases, much depends on how the previous owner(s) treated the youngster. His inherent nature is also a minimal factor. A puppy reared in a loving environment, free from any physical discipline, will be totally different from one where the owner was short tempered—too quick to use

Before a puppy is brought into your household, sit down with your family and discuss a puppy's training needs. Write these down so you will have a reminder, of what was agreed. The list should include behaviors deemed acceptable. This list will be a useful reference to check progress and highlight matters needing extra attention once the puppy arrives. It will also help you get more involved with the puppy, taking satisfaction from the results of your efforts.

Once the puppy does arrive, revise your training objectives as needed. Is their a special behavior in which your puppy needs extra attention? Paying close

Your puppy's temperament can be affected by his health. Owners of dogs with ear problems can choose from a variety of ear care products, from cleaners to remedies for proper ear hygiene. Photo courtesy of Four Paws.

punishment when the pup was other than an angel. A puppy raised in a kennel environment, where he had little contact with humans will lack the all important imprinting essential to a pup needing to socialize in a human world. He may not have received poor handling, but he will be nervous with people because he is unfamiliar with them. He may appear in some ways to be a formerly mistreated puppy.

The testing of puppies advocated by some trainers to establish a pup's personality—bold, shy, average and so on—are not as foolproof as they claim to be. They may be indicative of previous background, or health, as much as true character. It is better to assess what you have in front of you, than make an assumption that the pup has this or that nature and must always be treated on that basis. Your puppy is not unlike a child. What he is as a youngster can change dramatically by the time he is mature. The environment he lives in, and the way he is treated and trained, are the most influential factors in determining the adult he turns out to be.

DETERMINING TEMPERAMENT

The following questions and comments will serve as a guide in helping you determine what is and is not normal puppy behavior. They can not determine personality. Personality can only be assessed after any former bad experiences from the puppy's background have been neutralized. This allows inherent character to begin to

show through. Bonding will reveal personality, and harsh discipline and inconsistency in training will suppress personality.

The first question to ask yourself is: When first approached how did the puppy react to you? A normal reaction would consist of a puppy that came in a rush to your call with his tail held high and wagging and

launched himself at you. This puppy has been well socialized—the easiest dog to train. If a puppy approaches you cautiously, wagging his tail in a low position, rolls over in front of you, tries to retreat from you, or even urinates when you bend over him, this puppy exhibits fear probably due to previous mishandling. The puppy may have been isolated from

A puppy's temperament is very important in deciding what training methods you will use. Careful observation will determine your puppy's personality traits.

There are certain situations in which a puppy may be observed to determine his temperament. His reactions to a given situation will give you a good idea of his previous experiences.

humans, or had the lowest rank in his litter. A puppy of this sort will require extra patience and may be too much of a challenge for some owners. By all means, delay formal training until his fears have been assuaged.

Secondly, how does the puppy react when being lifted? A normal reaction for a young puppy will be to go limp initially and then wriggle, lick and try to smother you with affection. Pups instinctively go limp when their mother carries them. Once they feel secure their exuberance and lack of human fear is overtly displayed. This will surely be an easy pup to train. An abnormal reaction will be much the same as described

earlier. The puppy may cringe or urinate, he will not attempt to give you a wash. He may even stay motionless with his ears in a submissively low position. These behaviors also suggest previous mistreatment, he may have been mauled and dropped by children, and is now generally fearful.

When taken home how does the puppy react to various objects in the room? A well adjusted puppy will be curious but cautious. When he is unsure, he will look at an object with his ears and tail erect. He may growl, bark, or even jump in a playful manner around the object. A mal-adjusted puppy will be extremely cautious, and give a

wide birth to the object, possibly running from it. He may not have been in a home previously and is unfamiliar with household objects, or he associates with some previous mishandling, or the pup may have developed a nervous disposition due to poor socialization.

Now ask yourself, how does he react in your yard as opposed to your home? A normal puppy's reactions should be similar in both situations. He may show apprehension at passing vehicles, but should not be unduly frightened by them. Any undue apprehension may stem from simply having lived in a quieter location than your home.

A puppy that may have been poorly socialized will display nervousness or will run to a safe spot in an effort to hide. If he is more at ease outside than inside the house, he may have been reared in a kennel situation, and tend to lack sufficient socialization activities.

Finally, how does your puppy react to trash bins? Make this observation when the pup cannot see you. Most puppies show interest. A pup's scenting ability, added to his curiosity, usually make a trash bin an especially fascinating object. When you do reveal yourself to the puppy he will either carry on his investigation, or come over to you. Some puppies will show undue interest and less caution at trying to get at the contents. They will seem fearful when you show yourself, however, will return to the trash bin after he has been moved away from it. This

A curious puppy who reacts inquisitively, with an appropriate amount of caution to new situations has most likely been exposed to social situations.

A puppy that has been poorly socialized will often appear nervous and withdrawn in new situations.

pup may have lacked a correct diet in content or quantity. He has probably been physically punished for raiding the bin, thus his expression of fear when a human appears. You can assume he may have been punished for other puppy pranks that do not necessarily warrant this reaction.

The preceding situations will help you to gage your puppy's temperament as well as give you a good idea of the methods you should apply when training. Remember all animals are trainable. With the proper care your training will be successful. We recommend the following questions for use in the further evaluation of your puppy's needs.

Remember, all animals are trainable. Through persistence and care your training will be successful.

Keep in mind that the testing of puppies to determine personality—bold, shy, happy or reserved—is not fool proof. The results of the tests are only an indication of a puppy's disposition.

• How does he react to sporadic noises— vacuums, machines and the like?

• How does he react when you bend over him from the front?

• How does he react to other pets?

• When tired, where does he go to sleep? Does he try to be near to you or does he hide behind something?

DEALING WITH AN UNSOCIALIZED PUPPY

The worst thing you can do once you realize that your puppy is reacting abnormally would be to confront the puppy with the source of the problem and forcibly make him face it while trying to reassure him. At first, avoid the source of his anxiety when possible, for example remove the trash bin, and concentrate all your efforts into providing him with pleasurable situations. Your first concern is to win the puppy's trust— you can then deal with

problems one at a time as the bond between you grows. Most problems related to unfamiliarity of objects and places are relatively easy to deal with. They are cured in a natural manner by gradual familiarity. Problems having a basis in fear are the hardest

to overcome, but are by no means insurmountable. The degree of fear will be dependent on how deeply the problem situations have become rooted in the puppy's mind. However, with time, trust and consistent training, these too can be overcome.

All difficulties with training will be overcome in time. Your first and foremost concern is to win your puppy's trust. You can then confront any problems as the bond between the two of you grows.

If you realize that your puppy is poorly socialized the worst thing you can do is overwhelm him. At first, avoid the sources of his anxiety and concentrate all your efforts on providing him with a secure environment.

UNDERSTANDING BEHAVIOR

In this chapter you will come to understand some of the reasons your puppy behaves as he does. An understanding of behavior will make you more able to train him, and better qualified to pinpoint the sources of some common problems. We will explore patterns of behavior and their consequences. Unfortunately, in many cases, an owner who has no understanding of behavior will reinforce inappropriate behaviors through poor discipline techniques. Invariably they compound the problem and create confusion in the dog's mind.

Before we discuss the key aspects of pet psychology, there are two phrases that you should keep in mind: Violence (otherwise known as hard discipline) is never an option. Although it may overcome the immediate frustration of the owner, it never does anything to solve the dog's problem. The only certainty of inconsistent discipline is negative side effects. If you are not consistent in training, your dog will be inconsistent in his behavior.

PET PSYCHOLOGY

The first key aspect of pet psychology is reinforcement. Reinforcers are any stimuli serving to enforce a given behavior. A primary reinforcer is a stimuli, such as punishment, or petting, applied at the time of a behavior. A discriminatory reinforcer is a stimuli that replaces a primary enforcer, but has the same effect. It carries the implication of the primary. "No" and "Good boy" are the examples most commonly used. However, here the words are only part of the stimuli—the tone of voice, together with facial and body expressions, are equally as important. Your size,

Gaining an understanding of why your puppy behaves the way he does will make it easier to train him and pinpoint the sources of any difficulties.

Reinforcers are the first key aspect of psychology. A reinforcer can be positive or negative, either encouraging or discouraging behavior.

Generalization is one of the most difficult behaviors for a puppy to overcome because anything in the environment may become the source of a negative generalization. A watchful eye should prevent your puppy from encountering any situations in which this would be possible.

First you must remove the enforcer(s), making it more difficult for the puppy to engage in the activity. If that fails, make the desire to commit the act, less appealing than the consequence of actually doing it. Caught in the act or surprise discipline is ineffective. These methods will only work when you are present. Removal of the reinforcer is a guarantee of 100% success.

GENERALIZATION

Generalization may itself apply both positively and negatively. For example, your puppy goes to the vet and is subject to a painful treatment. The vet wears a white coat. Some days later you visit a friend who is wearing a white coat, and the puppy shows instant fear. The original source of the fear, the pain resulting from the treatment, at the vet's office, has been transferred in the pup's mind to color of the clothing. You might unwittingly chastise the pup for his fear of your friend. In so doing, you reinforce that fear.

Generalization is one of the singular most difficult behaviors to overcome because, anything in the environment may become a potential source of negative generalization. The best way to minimize the risk of negative generalizations is to try and ensure that the puppy is never placed in a situation that you know may result in fear. For example, do not wait until the puppy has a problem before visiting the vet. Take him in for a check-up, that way he'll become accustomed to the environment under generally non-stressful

coupled with the tone of your voice and facial expression, leave the youngster in no doubts about your meaning.

An internalized reinforcer is an action that serves to intensify a behavior without any need for additional reinforcement. The act itself is the reinforcer. Eating, breathing, sleeping, urinating, defecating, running, and the like are instinctive internal reinforcers. Acquired internal reinforcers may be called habits. An important distinction should be made between those needing discriminatory commands, such as: sit, heel, and stay, as opposed to true internal reinforcers, such as trash bin

raiding. In these instances the acts reinforce the behavior without their ever needing periodic support with enforcers. In the case of trash bin raiding, this may continue after the original cause— incorrect diet for example— has been rectified. The removal of the bin will help, but the need to rummage has become a behavior pattern and may be transferred to other things. The problem is not as simple as it may seem. The owner assumes the dog is after something specific, rather than a simple need to rummage, which presents a more difficult problem.

There are ways to overcome acquired internal reinforcers.

conditions. Therefore, when presented with a difficult situation the puppy will experience less anxiety and will not associate the veterinarian's office with pain and fear. Likewise, never take a puppy who is unfamiliar with the hustle and bustle of a busy town center into one without first getting him familiar with people and traffic under less busy conditions.

Everything is new to a puppy, by taking things slowly you are ensuring all the generalizations he makes will be of a positive nature.

SCHEDULE STRETCHING

Learned behaviors require reinforcement from time to time, that time is referred to as schedule stretching. Schedule stretching refers to the time lapse between instances of reinforcement. An example of this can be illustrated using the sit command. Once learned, there will come a time when the puppy does not sit when told, so you will need to repeat the command in a firmer voice. It may be days, weeks, or months since the behavior was learned. Even still, each behavior is variable, depending on the individual dog, and the behavior pattern under consideration. Remember, if the correct behavior gains something the dog enjoys, his schedule stretch will be far longer than

if the gain is minimal or nothing at all. Only very occasional use of the reinforcer will be needed to maintain this behavior.

It is important that you do not weaken in your resolve. If your dog is sleeping on the chair, sitting in the beg position to obtain something, nudging you while you are seated, or jumping up at you, his behavior must be corrected. Oftentimes, behaviors that will have comparatively short schedules (needing more regular reinforcers) will be those that involve restrictions to the dog—sit, stay, down, and heel. Here, regular practice of the action will be the constant reinforcer that removes the

Schedule stretching refers to the time lapse between instances of reinforcement. For example, once puppies, like these American Staffordshire Terriers, learn the sit-stay command they will occasionally need to be reminded of its meaning.

It is important to train puppies, like these Old English Sheepdogs, in quiet areas where their rather high threshold for distraction will not come into play.

threshold activities. Things such as patience—which are more difficult for a puppy to achieve—are considered high threshold. Hence, it is important to train a puppy in a quiet area where his rather high threshold for distraction won't come into play.

COUNTER CONDITIONING

Counter conditioning encourages a desired behavior while discouraging an unwanted one. It gives the puppy an alternate choice in a given situation. For example, your puppy nudges you to obtain attention. If you give in, the action will be reinforced. If allowed to continue, by the time the pup is an adult dog that same action will become a real nuisance. When applying counter conditioning you would say "Down" each time the puppy nudged you. Practiced consistently, the dog will eventually realize that nudging is an unwanted

need for the verbal command. Humane correction and insistence in obeying your house rules is not tyrannical, it simply helps your puppy to live by certain rules for his own good as well as that of the family.

THRESHOLDS

A threshold is the amount of stimulus required to elicit a response from your puppy. Understanding thresholds helps us to explain why some things are more difficult to teach a dog than others, thus requiring more patience. Thresholds range from low to high. A dog with a low threshold will require little stimuli to elicit a response. Many behaviors are variable. A hungry dog has a low threshold for eating, but as he eats the threshold rises, peaking when the dog is satiated. An underfed puppy is far more likely to start raiding trash bins than one

that is well fed. He needs to satiate his unsatisfied threshold levels.

Basically, things that come easily to a puppy such as chasing, jumping, and playing are considered to be low

Dental products available to fight plaque, reduce tartar build-up and control unpleasant breath, your puppy will love having his teeth brushed! Photo courtesy of Four Paws.

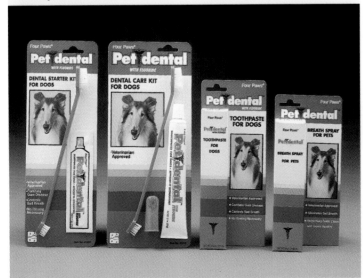

A puppy must always be able to control the outcome of his actions. Learned helplessness refers to the confusion created when an owner praises a puppy for an action and on another occasion disciplines the puppy for doing the same thing.

behavior that he gains nothing from—but laying down in front of you will get him attention.

LEARNED HELPLESSNESS

Learned helplessness refers to a situation of great

Counter conditioning allows your puppy to learn in a constructive manner which behaviors are appropriate and which are not.

confusion for a puppy. It is created when an owner disciplines a dog for doing something, but on another occasion praises the dog for doing exactly the same thing. A puppy must always be able to control the outcome of his actions. This means if you call the puppy to you praise him when he comes—obedience must never result in discipline. When an owner is inconsistent in his actions he leaves his dog in a situation where he just doesn't know what to do. The consequences may be an anxiety ridden dog who will react with stress and upset to any command.

APPLY WHAT YOU KNOW

Always decide in advance the training methods you will use, and reassess them again as training progresses. If you come up against a problem refer to these psychological terms to see if they can be of help in understanding what is affecting your puppy's

behavior. If you use your intellect, your growing understanding of your puppy's mind, and unlimited affection and patience, you can train your puppy without ever becoming frustrated. You will have the perfect canine companion, and he will have an owner he both respects and loves.

Always decide in advance which training methods you will apply and reassess them continually as training progresses.

HOUSEBREAKING

Housebreaking will most likely be your first training experience with your puppy.

Housebreaking and paper training are not difficult behaviors to teach your puppy, but they require consistency, and a high degree of patience. Some owners encounter problems with housebreaking because they do not understand all that's involved. Once problems become evident the owner either accepts the problem and continually chastises the dog, merely confusing it, or the poor pet is banished to an outdoor lifestyle. With the paper training techniques none of this will be necessary.

THE SOCIAL IMPORTANCE OF SCENTING

To humans, the removal of waste products from the body is purely a biological necessity. Although true of dogs, elimination has an extra, important role. Believe

it or not elimination serves as a prime means of communication. Males, in

particular, use urine as a means of marking their territory. This is called scent posting. It lets other dogs know they are present in the area. The scenting ability of dogs allows them to tell how recently the scent was deposited, whether it's from a male or female, and whether it's a dog they know, or a stranger. A female's scent tells males if she is in heat. Dogs also recognize their own scent, which is freshened on each visit to the same spot.

Dog stools perform a similar role, but because they are not deposited as frequently, urination is the prime communicator. You cannot, and should not, attempt to prevent this natural process and ability in

One of the fundamentals of housetraining is a designated potty spot—a place where your puppy knows he should go to relieve himself. And if that spot is easy to clean and use, the training will be easier for you and the pup. Photo courtesy of Puppy Go Potty™.

your puppy. Although it cannot be stopped, it is possible to control where the puppy attends to his biological needs. This is what housebreaking, or paper training, is all about.

The first concern in housebreaking is understanding your puppy's needs. These are related to his feeding times and play times, as well as when he naps. Remember a puppy does not have the same power to control his bowel movements as an older dog.

FEEDING SCHEDULE

Apart from being nutritionally sound, your puppy must be fed at regular times. During the housetraining period it is better to control water intake by supplying it at regular intervals, along with his meal.

One of the fundamentals of good health throughout your dog's life is a sound, healthy diet. Photo courtesy of Nutro Products, Inc.

The time at which unwanted waste leaves the body is determined by two factors. As food enters the digestive tract it accelerates the movement of food in the system, thus the need to release the waste products of the previous meal. If food enters one end at regular times the waste products will leave the other end at somewhat regular times. This will mostly be shortly after the intake of fresh food and water. Exactly how long after varies on an individual basis. Therefore, a predictable food-excrement pattern is created.

The second factor is that for a limited time, which increases with maturity, the dog is able, via musculature, to control when he releases his waste products. However, there is a limit to this time span of control. At such a point nature will not be stopped! If no pattern exists, the release of waste products

While we are discussing diet it is important to remember that we must keep our animal friends' teeth and gums healthy. Fortunately, maintaining oral care is getting easier and easier for pet owners. Now there's a taste-free, easy-to-use gel that will keep pets' teeth clean, reduce tartar build up and eliminate breath odor. Photo courtesy of Breath Friend™ American Media Group.

Remember, along with a proper feeding schedule, maturity and good health should also be a concern in your puppy's regimen.

will be on a schedule related to the irregular intake. The result will be apparent in irregular bowel movements. They are actually still regular in the biological time sequence, but unpredictable from your training standpoint.

A third factor that should be considered is health. If a puppy is ill this will interrupt normality, making bowel movements less predictable, and far less controllable.

CHOOSE YOUR METHOD

Although housebreaking and paper training achieve the same objective, they are different in a number of ways you should understand before deciding which is appropriate for your situation.

Housebreaking means the puppy is taught to attend to himself outside of your home. Paper training means the puppy will be trained to attend his needs indoors, in a particular spot, on paper. Although it is possible to paper train a puppy, then transfer him to outside, it often proves difficult. Housebreaking is the preferred method because it carries less risk of problems later on. However, circumstances may dictate paper training is more convenient for certain dogs under certain conditions, such as residence in a high rise apartment. If you plan to paper train, commence as soon as the pup is taken

home. If housebreaking, this should be delayed until the puppy's permanent inoculations are effective— usually by the age of 12 weeks. Until then restrict the pup's freedom to only those times when you are present and watching him.

PAPER TRAINING

Place sheets of paper at least two or three in thickness on an easy to clean floor, ensuring the entire surface is covered. When the puppy starts his relief ritual— turning in circles, whimpering, sniffing the floor, and stooping—place him on the paper designated to be his toilet area. Remember, he will need to relieve himself a short

Paper training and housebreaking are equally effective methods of teaching your puppy the appropriate places to relieve himself. They require consistency and a high degree of patience on the part of the owner.

time after he has eaten, drank, or been playing. Also, place him on the paper periodically anyway, this will increase the chances that you will get it right most of the time. If the puppy fouls another area of the paper it's okay. Take the part of the paper that's stained and place it under the sheet you want the puppy to use. He will usually sniff out this spot the next time. It may take a few tries before the spot is used regularly.

If you catch the pup relieving himself other than on the paper, go to him swiftly, lift him up, say nothing and place him on the desired spot. If he completes his needs lavish him with praise. You are teaching by encouraging the desired behavior rather than disciplining the unwanted behavior—a powerful difference in your psychological approach.

Once the puppy has been successful a few times, reduce about 25% of the papered area and continue as discussed. If success is still maintained remove another 25% the next day, and so on until the only papered area is the one it is now using. If an occasional error is made on the non-papered floor wipe up and clean thoroughly. If there are many errors go back to the original stage and start again. It is frustrating, but is the only way to attain lasting success. Do not give the puppy other room access and freedom until he's fully paper trained. Paper training should normally be complete within about 5-7 days, but allow for the slower learner.

Accidents will happen. All you can do is be prepared by being armed with a non-toxic, effective stain and odor remover. Photo courtesy of Francodex.

HOUSEBREAKING

When you first take puppy home give him a few minutes in your yard to attend to his biological needs, praising him when he does so. From this point, until his inoculations are effective, proceed with caution, as discussed earlier. Once you are ready to begin housebreaking, take the puppy outdoors to a designated area, shortly after it has been fed. Allow him to exercise for about 10-15 minutes, during which he will wish to relieve himself. Once he does, lavish him with praise. The benefit of having familiarized the puppy with his collar and lead will be appreciated at this time. It will enable you to restrict exercise to the specific area you wish the puppy to relieve himself in. It's important you take the puppy out after every meal in order to reinforce this behavior pattern. If your puppy will attend to his needs in the street you should go prepared. A scoop and

Housebreaking can be made easier with pads that are scientifically treated to attract puppies when nature calls. The plastic lining prevents damage to floors and carpets. Photo courtesy of Four Paws.

container can be purchased from your pet shop. Always clean up after your pet.

Any accidents in the home during this period must be overlooked and dealt with in the neutral manner discussed, chastising your puppy will only confuse him. You must watch at this time for any signs that the puppy wishes to go out. Make sure to praise him for his efforts. However, if the puppy persists in using the home, as well as the yard, first examine your habits. Are you not feeding at a regular time? If you catch the puppy in the act once he is familiar with using the yard, go straight to him and say no in a firm, but not overwhelming, tone. Take him outside immediately, praising him if he relieves himself.

At no time during housebreaking or paper training should you rub the pup's nose in his excrement. This achieves nothing except

to weaken the bond between owner and puppy, who doesn't connect the nose rubbing with something he shouldn't do. It does, however, increase the potential for the puppy to develop coprophagia—a syndrome in which he starts to eat his own fecal matter. He is encouraged in this behavior by the fact that his owner is forcing his nose into the excrement. Never, in matters relating to bowel movements spank or loudly shout at the puppy. The fact that he runs

away does not mean he understands he is being disciplined for fouling the carpet. He thinks it means he is being disciplined for actually attending his needs. The next time, he will try another spot, and so on. By this method you are actually encouraging, by fear and confusion, the dog to foul more spots in your home. The answer is to start training again from the beginning. Losing your temper achieves nothing, using psychology achieves all objectives.

At no time during housebreaking should you chastise your puppy. Lavish him with praise for even the smallest success.

Any accidents that occur in the home should be overlooked in the beginning stages of training.

BASIC TRAINING COMMANDS

Formal training should not commence until a puppy is at least eight weeks old and fully settled into your home. He should be relaxed, and in good health. You cannot take him outside for training until his permanent inoculations are effective. You will be able to teach the sit, stay and down commands in your home, heel will follow shortly thereafter.

Some things to remember:

• Never make training sessions too long—a puppy's concentration is short. Limit sessions to a few minutes. But you can have 2-3 sessions a day.

• Never attempt training if you're not in a good mood. The moment you feel frustrated end the lesson, or take a few moments to gather your composure.

• Always end lessons with success, not failure. It doesn't matter what that success is, only that the puppy realizes it has pleased you and gained praise.

• Discipline teaches a puppy only what is not wanted rather than what is. This is only learned by successes. Always place the most emphasis on what the puppy does right, not what it does wrong. Praise should be lavish, discipline and corrections minimal.

• Training sessions should be free of distractions. As the puppy becomes more advanced, move into situations where there are distractions. The puppy learns, by degrees, to cope with these.

• Remember, your puppy is an individual—some are more placid or shy than others, and will need a softer tone of voice and greater patience.

• Do not hold training sessions immediately after your puppy has eaten, or been playing, but shortly before.

Formal training should not commence until a puppy is at least eight weeks old and fully settled into your home. He should be relaxed like these Pulis and in good health.

THE SIT

Kneel down and call the puppy to you. Place him in front of you with one hand on his chest, the other over his hindquarters. Apply gentle pressure to the hindquarters, at the same time saying "Sit" in a clear, firm tone. Praise him lavishly when he is seated. Move to another spot and repeat the exercise. However, do not repeat the exercise too many times in one session or the puppy will get bored. Repeated over a day or two, at regular intervals, the pup will soon be proficient in this command.

Once the puppy is obeying the command, call him to you and stand in front of him, rather than kneel. Practice till the puppy is proficient. Finally, repeat the exercise while you are seated in a chair. Using this three stage process (kneeling, standing, and sitting) the puppy is taught to obey the sit command regardless of your

This Afghan Hound is ready and willing to learn all you have to teach him!

position. He will eventually take up this position whenever he is called to you, not even needing the actual command.

SIT-STAY COMMAND

Only when the sit command is understood should you move to the sit-stay. A six foot lead will be useful. Place the puppy in front of you and use the sit command. Now move

Your puppy will find the Sit one of the easiest commands to master. Remember, practice makes perfect.

backwards a few feet. As you go say "Sit," at the same time hold your right hand in front of the puppy's face, palm forward. The moment the pup attempts to follow you, repeat the command. If it is ignored do not continue to use the command. Rather, say nothing and move towards the puppy. Repeat the sit command. Now start backwards again, repeating the original sequence. Note that no discipline or

This Chesapeake Bay Retriever awaits his next command from the sit-stay position.

corrections are used. Repetition, patience and praise for success, are much better methods to use. Once you can move backwards to the length of the lead with success every time, you can then walk forwards, turning your palm to face the dog as you say the command and begin to move. When this is achieved, walk back to the dog, and praise him. The final step is to walk to the end of the lead, turn, call the pup to you and give him the sit command. End with lavish praise.

Once able to perform this sequence you can sit the dog and walk around him, giving the stay command as you circle him. This achieved, you can try the command without the lead, increasing the distance between you and the dog. At this level keep the dog in the sit and stay position for a few seconds before calling him to you. The number of seconds can increase with success.

Looks like these Dalmatians are "so happy together" in the sit position.

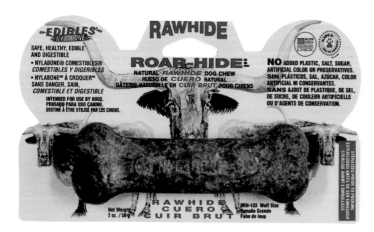

To combat boredom and relieve your puppy's natural desire to chew, there is nothing better than a Roar-Hide™. Unlike common rawhide, this bone won't turn into a gooey mess when chewed on. The Roar-Hide™ is completely edible, high in protein and low in fat. Roar-Hide™ is just right for your puppy. Available at your local pet shop.

An extra comment is now appropriate. In any training session always note the position of your puppy's ears. They may momentarily be laid flat against the head when a command is given, expressing subordination, but should return to their normal position. If they remain flat, and the puppy displays a cowering head action you are being too overbearing with a timid pup. Ease up on your voice tone and general demeanor, while increasing the praise.

THE DOWN COMMAND

This command is initially difficult for most dogs to accept because it's a very submissive position for them to assume. The bolder puppy will display the most resistance. Once he realizes there are no negative effects, the puppy will accept the command like any other.

There are a number of techniques used by trainers to teach this command: they fall into two basic categories. There are those where pressure on the lead, underneath the puppy's neck, forces him to the ground, and there are the paw and leg methods which involve pulling the front legs forward while

applying some pressure to the shoulders. In the paw method, the accompanying hand signal must be taught after the down command is understood. This author prefers the paw method because it usually encounters the least resistance, and it is a less threatening action to a puppy.

First, place the puppy in the sit-stay position, on his lead, next to your left leg. Kneel down and hold the lead in your left hand while placing the same hand over the puppy's shoulders. With a large breed you may need to bend your left arm and lay this across his shoulders with your wrist above the puppy's neck. The right hand grasps the pup's legs about mid way from the paws. Pulling the legs forward, and with slight pressure on the shoulders, the puppy is unable to resist and goes down (with the neck pressure method he can brace his legs and resist,

Your puppy will be happier and his teeth and gums healthier, if you give him a POPpup™ to chew on. Every POPpup™ is 100% edible and enhanced with dog friendly ingredients like liver, cheese, spinach, chicken, carrots, or potatoes. What you won't find in a POPpup™ is salt, sugar, alcohol, plastic or preservatives. You can even microwave a POPpup™ to turn it into a huge, crackly treat for your puppy to enjoy.

Praising your puppy is exceptionally important in all training sessions. Always end each lesson on a positive note.

which is not good for a puppy). Give the down command as you pull the legs forward. Once down, release and praise the puppy. Repeat the sequence a number of times before trying the pup without pulling his legs, simply applying pressure to his shoulders. Always praise after each success. Finally, try giving the command without applying any pressure. Once successful, move to the front of the puppy. Repeat the command, but commence by raising your hand, palm forward. As you say "Down," bring your hand down as well, so it arcs to end up horizontal to the floor. If the puppy does not go down, grasp the lead about four inches from the collar and gently pull downwards.

The fact that the puppy succeeded when you left his side means that little downward pressure will be required to remind him what he's supposed to do. If he still resists, return to the side position and start again. After success, remain in the same position and use the downward pull on the lead method, coupled with the hand signal. If this works, move to the front and repeat the sequence.

As with the sit-stay, progress by moving backwards away from the puppy and giving him the down command. Soon, you will be able to sit the puppy from a distance, then down him in successive commands. If the puppy starts to crawl towards you in the down position give the command "Stay." If this is ignored, go to the puppy and take it back to where he started and begin

again. Do not allow forward crawling—this is not obeying the stay command. There can be no half way measures: commands are either obeyed, or they are not. If he gets away with crawling forward he will soon enough start to slink forward.

Once the puppy

Products that help eliminate bad breath for your pet are widely available at pet shops. The one shown here is chewable and works with the digestive system to help neutralize your pet's bad breath. Photo courtesy of Four Paws.

performs the down command every time, you can slowly build up the time he stays in position. Do not, however, expect a young puppy to stay in any position for more than a few minutes. Your puppy's ability to do this will develop as he matures, and with regular practice.

The down command is the most difficult for puppies to master because it is such a submissive position. However, these Border Collie puppies don't seem to mind!

Before attempting to teach the heel command, all other problems must be eliminated. Be sure your puppy is comfortable wearing his collar and lead.

What You Will Need

A six foot lead is recommended. A choke chain, pronged or smooth, is preferable to a normal collar. Choose medium to large links appropriate for the size of your breed. You must be sure a choke chain is always on the right way, otherwise the rapid release of choke action will not happen. Pronged chokes seem rather fearsome, but in actuality are the best if viewed from a rapid result standpoint. Their appearance is the singular reason why pet owners view them as being cruel devices. Whatever choke you choose be sure it's the correct size. It should slip over the pup's head easily, yet not fall over his ears when slack.

At this age it is sufficient if he is able to perform all the basic commands in a proficient manner, having received a minimal amount of correction, and maximum praise, in learning them. If your puppy seems obstinate, or slow to learn, there is no need to become frustrated. It simply means the puppy clearly does not understand what's expected of him. Repetition and praise, which teach what is required, are always better when applied to learning, as opposed to discipline, which is more effective when applied to unwanted behaviors.

HEEL

Heel work is not easy for a puppy to perform and should not be attempted until he is about three months old. It requires more concentration and self control than a younger puppy will normally have. If the puppy is older than this upon his arrival, teach him the other commands first. They pave the way for this exercise, which incorporates each of the other command positions.

Preparing For Heel Work

The considerate trainer will minimize heel work problems by eliminating them beforehand. All unnecessary

The heel command requires more concentration and self-control than a young puppy usually has. It involves training your puppy to walk directly beside you on lead.

fear should be removed so the puppy only has to contend with learning this command. The puppy should be familiar with wearing his choke chain. It should not come as a sudden and frightening experience on the first day of heel training. In familiarizing the puppy to the choke chain

it should be used indoors, but never left on an unattended puppy. Walk around the home, or yard, so the puppy will understand its effect, but in a gentle manner. Encourage the puppy to walk with you so he does not lag behind. A choke is basically designed for use with a dog

moving forward, rather than pulling back. You do not want a lagging puppy when you start heel training. Do not attempt training until the pup is quite confident at walking with you. Do not use the heel command until you are ready to train and want it obeyed. You should also familiarize the puppy with the area you plan to train in. Select a quiet location with no distractions. Having a wall to walk beside is helpful. It enables you to adjust the lateral distance the puppy has to move away from your left leg.

Commencing Heel Training

The correct way to hold a lead is to place its handle over your right thumb. You can then gather up the slack, which is also held in your right hand at about waist level. Your left hand loosely holds the lead so it can be used for corrections. The puppy should be near your left leg in the sit position. His head should be in line with your knee. You lead off with your left leg. Say the dog's name followed by "Heel" in a firm, clear voice, then start forward. The heel command is important to emphasize.

Do not wait for the puppy to move on your command before you do. One of two things will now happen. The pup will start forward once its sees your left leg moving, or he will stay in the sit position. If he remains seated give one short jerk and let out the lead, but keep moving, and stop after a couple of steps. Do not go backwards to the puppy: call him to you.

Take up the slack in the lead and repeat the sequence several times. The puppy

Your puppy must understand the meaning of "No!" before he can master other commands.

If your think your dog has a future in the show ring, make sure he masters the heel command as a puppy.

should begin to get the message. A puppy will only lag behind if he has never been outside before, if the training area in some way frightens it, if he is nervous or timid, is unfamiliar with his collar and lead, or fearful of his owner. Hopefully, the lagging problem will not be an issue. If it is, end the lesson on an upbeat note and put in more practice walking the puppy on the choke.

Once on the move, the puppy will want to get ahead of you: this is when the correction must take place. As soon as the pup forges a foot or so ahead give a quick, sharp, backward jerk on the lead and say "Heel" in a firm voice. There is no need to let the puppy get well ahead and then bring him to a very abrupt stop by a sudden hard jerk, or turning and walking in the opposite direction. Time is not your enemy. You will achieve success in a series of small progressions, rather than by quantum leaps involving heavy handed methods. This said, the backward jerk must be meaningful, the command calm, but firm. It is not an option, but a command. Any tendency for the puppy to move away from your leg, should be prevented from the outset by short inward jerks on the lead—no command is necessary. This is where having a wall to walk along is helpful. By moving closer to this the puppy has no option but to stay where you want him in relation to your leg. Once the puppy is walking to heel in a straight line, every time, move on to the next stage.

Directional Changes
Commence walking forward with the puppy in the heel position. After a number of yards turn 45 degrees to your right. If the puppy has not noticed your directional change the subsequent quick inward jerk on the lead will

These two bright pupils eagerly await their next command.

Each command must be mastered before introducing the next. This Bloodhound looks pretty comfortable in the sit position.

command his attention. With some pups, a repeat of the heel command may be necessary, with others it may not. Ideally, avoid using excessive commands, let the corrections impart the message. Repeat this sequence a number of times until successful.

You are now ready to move through a 90 degree turn using the same method. By this stage the puppy will be aware he must keep near your left leg, and be attentive to the possibility of a directional change. His mind will be more focused. Practice until your turns are excellent, then

progress to complete about-face turns. Finally, do complete circle turns so the puppy learns to stay near your left leg at all times. The left turn presents a different problem. Here, the dog may be in the way as you change direction. In this case you should keep walking and your leg will make contact with the puppy. Do not try to avoid this contact. Some things in life are only learned by one's own mistakes: for the puppy this is one of those times. Do not expect obedience ring precision with a puppy. That will come with maturity and practice. But you do want

proficiency. If you allow your puppy to get in the habit of moving too far from your left leg there will come a time when this creates a problem. A post, a tree, or a person will end up between you and the puppy. For this reason it's essential, throughout the training of the heel command, that the puppy never be allowed to be more than nine inches from your leg.

THE COME TO HEEL COMMAND

The come to heel command is generally used when a puppy is off lead. The objective is, when called to

Before attempting the come to heel command off lead, be sure your puppy has mastered the command while still working on lead.

The come to heel command is generally used when a puppy is off lead. Once learned, the puppy will come from a distance and sit in front of you when called.

Now that they have mastered the sit-stay command, these American Eskimo puppies just have to learn to keep their elbows off the dinner table!

Once your puppy has been trained in the basic commands of sit, stay, down and heel they should be practiced and maintained on a daily basis.

A puppy receiving two to three short training sessions each day, should be proficient within three to six weeks.

you, the puppy will come and sit in front of you. On the command "Heel," he will pass on your right side, around your back, and sit in the heel position against your left leg. Teach this only after all other commands.

Using a six foot lead, sit and stay the dog in front of you at the end of the lead. Call the puppy to you and sit him in front of you. Next, give the heel command, at the same time pulling the puppy to your right so he passes around your back and into the heel position. As he does, you will pass the lead from your right to left hand, and then back to the right hand. It will take a few repeats before the puppy understands what's required. In all heel exercises you can use your left hand to encourage the puppy to stay near you. Periodically, lightly

slap your left thigh and give an inward tug on the lead with your right hand.

When the puppy has learned heel work on a lead it can be practiced with no lead. However, this takes a very well trained puppy and should not be attempted until the pup has mastered the command on lead. Even when a dog is an "old hand" at heel work you should always keep him on lead in streets and shopping centers.

Once your puppy has been trained in the key disciplines of sit, stay, down, and heel work these should be maintained on a daily basis. Do not allow them to become commands obeyed sometimes and not others. As the puppy becomes more advanced, take him to busier places where there are distractions so he learns to cope with these. All

forms of advanced dog training require that the commands discussed in this book can be performed proficiently. They are the ABC's of dog training. The speed at which your puppy learns these commands will be determined by the number of regular training sessions given.

As a guide, a puppy receiving two to three short sessions each day should be proficient within three to six weeks. This is not a lot of time to invest for a lifetime of having a well behaved dog that's a pleasure to live with.

ALTERNATIVES TO TRADITIONAL TRAINING METHODS

Most training classes you attend or books you read will advise you to train your dog using a nylon or metal

"Could you repeat that please?" It may take a few repeats before your puppy understands what is required of him.

The speed at which your puppy learns commands will be determined by the number of regular training sessions he participates in.

"choke"—a collar that tightens when you pull on the lead and loosens when you don't. The variable pressure lets your dog know if you want him to stop or not. But let's face it, not all dogs respond to this pressure. It can depend on how the trainer is applying it (and this can be too rough as well as too gentle), what the dog's motivation is at the time of the correction, and whether the dog has a particularly thick neck. For these reasons and more, despite your best efforts, you may not get the results you desire if you use this standard training equipment.

You may want to explore using a headcollar instead. Unlike a collar that wraps around the neck, a headcollar has two components: a nose loop that fits across the base of the muzzle, and a neck strap that fits high at the top of the neck. These work together via a leash that attaches under the dog's muzzle. The positions of the straps work to communicate leadership and reassurance. Just as a pack leader will firmly grasp a subordinate's muzzle in his mouth to reprimand him, so the nose strap lets your dog know you're the boss. And have you noticed how puppies relax when their mothers pick them up by the back of the neck? The neck strap on the headcollar has the same effect.

The nice thing about working a puppy in the headcollar is that he will learn to accept it faster and easier, so you won't have to retrain your dog when the standard methods fail.

Puppies, like these German Shepherds, are playful and energetic and need to be provided with ample opportunities for play breaks during training.

Don't rush your puppy's training. As anxious as you may be to have a properly trained companion, your puppy's early months are meant for play and flowers and sun. This tiny St. Bernard puppy is still enjoying the good life.

DEALING WITH PROBLEMS

If you diligently follow the advice given throughout this book you should not experience problems with the dog your puppy grows up to be. Almost every problem seen in dogs can be traced to a failure in training. If you find a problem is emerging, read this book again and try to pinpoint the cause. The answer may be to go back to basics. Establish your own authority and re-train the dog. Let him meet people and lead a normal dog's life.

Almost every problem seen in adult dogs can be traced to a failure in training. Puppies, like these Beagles, given consistent training early on will grow up to be exemplary canine citizens.

Why would you want to give your puppy a CARROT BONE™? Because you know carrots are rich in fiber, carbohydrates and vitamin A. Because it's a durable chew containing no plastics or artificial ingredients of any kind. Because it can be served as-is, in a bone-hard form or microwaved to a biscuit consistency—whichever your puppy prefers. Because it's a 100%-natural plaque, obesity and boredom fighter for your puppy. Available at your local pet shop.

ELECTRONIC TRAINING AIDS

In this high tech world electronic training aids are growing in numbers. There are collars that trigger mild shocks when the dog passes over hidden wires, that give shocks when remotely triggered by the owner, and electronic devices that activate if the dog gets near to anything you don't want him to go near.

More than anything, they are made for the owner who is unprepared to apply patience and sound training techniques. Many have potential negative side effects if not used skillfully.

Before you consider using training aids of this type, this author strongly recommends you to join a dog training class so your problems can be discussed with an expert.

At the end of the day the only really lasting way to own a delightful dog is to train him while he's young. Build on your relationship through affection, patience, and consistent and kind discipline.

This beautiful Bearded Collie takes a break from training to pose for the camera.

Your young puppy glows with potential and intelligence. This handsome litter of Jacquet Boxers, bred by Richard Tomita, promises future owners years of quality companionship.

More than anything else, your puppy wants to make you happy. By spending the time to train him while he is young, you are ensuring that the two of you will enjoy many happy days to come.

SUGGESTED READING

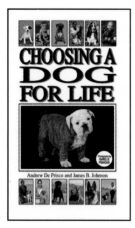

TS-257
Choosing a Dog for Life
By Andrew De Prisco &
Isabelle Francais
382 pages, over 700 color
photographs.

TS-214
Owner's Guide to Dog
Health
By Lowell Ackerman, DVM
432 pages, over 300 color
photographs

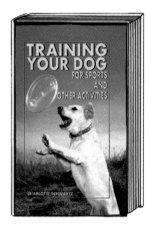

TS-258
Training Your Dog For
Sports and Other Activities
By Charlotte Schwartz
160 pages, over 100 color
photographs

TS-197
The World of the Golden
Retriever
By Nona Kilgore Bauer
480 pages, over 700 color
photographs

TS-293
Adopting a Great Dog:
Guide to Rehoming a
Rescue or Shelter Dog
By Nona Kilgore Bauer
128 pages, over 100 color
photographs

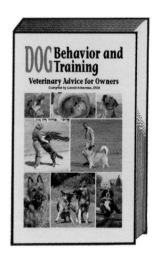

TS-252
Dog Behavior and Training:
Veterinary Advice for
Owners
Compiled by Dr. Lowell
Ackerman
288 pages, over 200 color
photographs